Acid Reflux Cookbook

MAIN COURSE - Delicious Breakfast
recipes and Vegetarian Recipes Easy to
Prepare for Health improvement
(GERD and LPR approach)

TABLE OF CONTENTS

This document is geared towards providing exact and reliable information in regards to the topic and issue covered. The publication is sold with the idea that the publisher is not required to render accounting, officially permitted, or otherwise, qualified services. If advice is necessary, legal or professional, a practiced individual in the profession should be ordered.

- From a Declaration of Principles which was accepted and approved equally by a Committee of the American Bar Association and a Committee of Publishers and Associations.

any type of guarantee assurance.

Introduction

Acid reflux recipes for family and personal enjoyment. You will love them for how easy it is to prepare them.

APPLE CINNAMON BREAD

Serves: **8**
Prep Time: **20** minutes
Cook Time: **95** minutes
Total Time: **115** minutes

INGREDIENTS

- ¼ cup pecans (coarsely chopped)
- ¼ salt
- 2 cups apples
- ½ low fat buttermilk
- ½ tablespoon pure vanilla extract
- 2 tablespoons canola oil
- ¼ wheat germ
- 2 tablespoons baking powder
- ½ tablespoon baking powder
- ½ tablespoon ground cinnamon
- 3 large egg whites
- 1 ¼ cups all purpose white flour
- ¾ cup whole wheat flour
- 2/3 cup Z-Sweet stevia
- ½ cup unsweetened applesauce

- 3 tablespoons maple syrup
- ¼ tsp ground cinnamon
- 1 large egg yolk

DIRECTIONS

1. Preheat oven to 350 F.
2. Line a 1 ½ quart glass Pyrex oblong loaf pan with foil.
3. Combine the pecans, maple syrup and cinnamon in a small bowl.
4. Whisk egg yolk, canola oil, Z-sweet and vanilla extract.
5. Whisk the egg whites until they begin to be frothy and white.
6. Place the all-purpose flour, salt, baking powder, cinnamon and baking soda in a sifter and sift into a mixing bowl.
7. Pour the batter into the lined Pyrex dish, spread the pecan and maple syrup mixture evenly over the top and place in the preheated oven.

Nutritional Facts

Amount Per Serving		
Calories 197	Calories from Fat 39	
	% Daily Value	
Total Fat 5g		7%

Saturated Fat 1g		3%
Monounsaturated Fat 2g		
Trans Fat 0g		
Cholesterol 27mg		9%
Sodium 309mg		13%
Total Carbohydrates 33g		11%
Dietary Fiber 3g		14%
Sugars 6g		
Protein 6g		
Vitamin A 1%	Vitamin C 2%	
Calcium 11%	Iron 11%	
Vitamin K 1 mcg	Potassium 200 mg	
Magnesium 37 mg		

BANANA BUT BREAD

Serves: **8**
Prep Time: **15**   minutes
Cook Time: **95**   minutes
Total Time: **110**   minutes

INGREDIENTS

- 1 egg yolk
- ½ cup pecans
- 1 tablespoon canola oil
- ½ tablespoon ground cinnamon
- ¼ tablespoon ground nutmeg
- 2 bananas
- 3 large egg whites
- 1 ¼ white flour
- ¼ cup wheat germ
- 3 tablespoons baking powder
- ½ tablespoon vanilla extract
- ½ baking soda
- ¼ low-fat buttermilk
- 1 ½ tablespoons brown sugar
- 2/3 cup Z-Sweet stevia

- ¼ tablespoon salt

DIRECTIONS

1. Preheat oven to 350 F.
2. Line a 1 ½ quart glass Pyrex oblong loaf pan with foil.
3. Whisk the egg yolk and add canola oil.
4. Mash the bananas into the mixture, add vanilla extract, Z-Sweet and whisk them.
5. Whisk the egg whites and they are frothy and white.
6. Add into a mixing bowl wheat flour, baking powder, salt, baking soda, cinnamon, wheat germ and nutmeg and sift them.
7. Fold the creamed mixture together with the flour mixture.
8. Add buttermilk and fold them.
9. Pour the batter into the lined Pyrex dish and sprinkle the brown sugar over the top.

Nutritional Facts

Amount Per Serving

Calories 225	Calories from Fat 59
	% Daily Value

Total Fat 7g	11%
Saturated Fat 1g	4%
Monounsaturated Fat 4g	
Trans Fat 0g	
Cholesterol 27mg	9%
Sodium 301mg	13%
Total Carbohydrates 36g	12%
Dietary Fiber 4g	16%
Sugars 6g	
Protein 7g	
Vitamin A 1%	Vitamin C 5%
Calcium 10%	Iron 11%
Vitamin K 1 mcg	Potassium 269 mg
Magnesium 50 mg	

BANANA NUT MUFFINS

Serves: **6**
Prep Time: **5**   minutes
Cook Time: **25**   minutes
Total Time: **30**   minutes

INGREDIENTS

- 1 large egg
- ½ white flour
- ½ wheat flour
- 3 tablespoons wheat germ
- ¼ salt
- 1 tablespoon canola oil
- ¼ tablespoon ground nutmeg
- ¼ cup low-fat buttermilk
- 3 tablespoons brown sugar
- 1 banana
- ½ tablespoon vanilla extract
- 1 tablespoon baking powder
- ¼ tablespoon baking soda
- ½ tablespoon ground cinnamon
- ½ Z-Sweet Stevia

- 1/2 cup pecans

DIRECTIONS

1. Preheat oven to 350 F.
2. Use a whisk and cream together the egg yolk.
3. Add banana and mash into the mixture.
4. Add vanilla extract and blend.
5. Fold in the chopped pecans.
6. Sift the whole wheat flour, baking powder, salt, baking soda, wheat germ, cinnamon and nutmeg.
7. Fold mixture together with the flour mixture.
8. Whisk the egg white until is white and foamy.
9. Fold in the buttermilk and the dough.
10. Line a standard size muffin tin with 7 papers and fill each muffin paper with equal amount of batter.

Nutritional Facts

Amount Per Serving

Calories 205	Calories from Fat 54
	% Daily Value
Total Fat 6g	10%
Saturated Fat 1g	4%
Monounsaturated Fat 3g	
Trans Fat 0g	

Cholesterol 33mg		12%
Sodium 251mg		10%
Total Carbohydrates 32g		11%
Dietary Fiber 3g		13%
Sugars 5g		
Protein 6g		
Vitamin A 1%		Vitamin C 3%
Calcium 8%		Iron 10%
Vitamin K 2 mcg		Potassium 205 mg
Magnesium 35 mg		

BLUEBERRY MUFFIN

Serves: **6**
Prep Time: **15**   minutes
Cook Time: **25**   minutes
Total Time: **40**   minutes

INGREDIENTS

- 2 tablespoons yogurt
- ½ wheat flour
- ½ tablespoon vanilla extract
- ½ cup low-fat buttermilk
- ½ blueberries
- 1 cup white flour
- 2 tablespoons canola oil
- ¼ tablespoon salt
- 2 tablespoons baking powder
- ¼ tablespoon baking soda
- ½ cup Sweet Stevia
- 1 egg
- 2 tablespoons wheat germ

DIRECTIONS

1. Preheat over to 375 F.
2. Separate egg into an egg white and egg yolk and set egg yolk aside.
3. Whisk the egg white.
4. Cream together egg yolk and canola oil and add sweet stevia and vanilla extract.
5. Mix wheat flour, salt, wheat germ, flour, baking powder and baking soda in a sifter and sift into a bowl.
6. Fold the creamed mixture together with the flour mixture.
7. Blend the mixture and add buttermilk.
8. Froth the egg whites until white and fold them into the batter.
9. Line a muffin tin with muffin papers and fill each muffin paper with equal amount of batter.

Nutritional Facts

Amount Per Serving	
Calories 163	Calories from Fat 27
	% Daily Value
Total Fat 3g	5%
Saturated Fat 1g	3%

Monounsaturated Fat 1g	
Trans Fat 0g	
Cholesterol 39mg	12%
Sodium 265mg	11%
Total Carbohydrates 26g	9%
Dietary Fiber 2g	10%
Sugars 3g	
Protein 7g	
Vitamin A 1%	Vitamin C 2%
Calcium 9%	Iron 10%
Vitamin K 4 mcg	Potassium 134 mg
Magnesium 32 mg	

RAISIN BRAN MUFFINS

Serves: **6**
Prep Time: **20**   minutes
Cook Time: **45**   minutes
Total Time: **65**   minutes

INGREDIENTS

- 1 cup raisins
- 1 ½ tablespoon canola oil
- 1 ½ cups fiber cereal
- ¼ tablespoon salt
- ½ tablespoon ground nutmeg
- 3 egg whites
- ½ cup unsweetened applesauce
- ½ cup stevia
- 2/3 cup flour
- ½ 2% milk
- ¼ cup low-fat buttermilk
- 1 egg yolk
- 2/3 wheat flour
- 2 tablespoons baking powder
- ¼ baking soda

DIRECTIONS

1. Preheat oven to 375 F.

2. Cream together the canola oil and egg yolk until smooth.

3. Add Stevia and unsweetened applesauce and whisk until smooth.

4. Sift wheat flour, baking powder, flour, baking soda, salt and nutmeg into a bowl.

5. Add raisins over the top of the flour mixture and fold the raisin and flour mixture together.

6. Whisk the egg whites until white.

7. Fold the egg whites into the muffin mixture until they are blended.

8. Line a standard size muffin tin with 7 muffin papers and fill each muffin paper with equal amount of mixture.

Nutritional Facts

Amount Per Serving

Calories 266	Calories from Fat 28
	% Daily Value
Total Fat 3g	5%
Saturated Fat 1g	4%
Monounsaturated Fat 1g	

Trans Fat 0g		
Cholesterol 37mg		12%
Sodium 335mg		14%
Total Carbohydrates 59g		20%
Dietary Fiber 10g		42%
Sugars 20g		
Protein 9g		
Vitamin A 2%	Vitamin C 7%	
Calcium 16%	Iron 23%	
Vitamin K 2 mcg	Potassium 456 mg	
Magnesium 56 mg		

CARROT MUFFINS

Serves: **6**
Prep Time: **5**   minutes
Cook Time: **25** minutes
Total Time: **30** minutes

INGREDIENTS

- 3 tablespoons yogurt
- 1 egg
- 1 tablespoon baking powder
- ¼ salt
- ½ tablespoon vanilla extract
- 1 cup white flour
- ½ tablespoon cinnamon
- ¼ tablespoon baking soda
- ¼ nutmeg
- 1 cup carrots
- 2 tablespoons canola oil
- ¼ cup oatmeal
- ½ cup sweet stevia
- ½ cup low-fat buttermilk
- ½ cup wheat flour

DIRECTIONS

1. Preheat oven to 375 F.

2. Separate the egg into an egg white and egg yolk and set aside the egg yolk.

3. Add canola oil, sweet stevia, egg yolk, vanilla extract and canola oil and mix whisk together until smooth.

4. Add flour, wheat flour, baking soda, baking powder, cinnamon and nutmeg in a sifter and sift into a bowl.

5. Fold the creamed mixture together with the flour and oatmeal.

6. Slowly add carrots and start blending them.

7. Add buttermilk until smooth and stop when is completely blended.

8. Line a muffin tin with muffin papers and fill each muffin paper with an equal amount of batter.

Nutritional Facts

Amount Per Serving	
Calories 175	Calories from Fat 29
	% Daily Value
Total Fat 3g	5%
Saturated Fat 1g	3%

Monounsaturated Fat 2g	
Trans Fat 0g	
Cholesterol 36mg	12%
Sodium 275mg	12%
Total Carbohydrates 30g	10%
Dietary Fiber 3g	12%
Sugars 3g	
Protein 7g	
Vitamin A 62%	Vitamin C 2%
Calcium 10%	Iron 11%
Vitamin K 4 mcg	Potassium 213 mg
Magnesium 38 mg	

CORNBREAD MUFFINS

Serves: *12*
Prep Time: *15*   minutes
Cook Time: *25*   minutes
Total Time: *40*   minutes

INGREDIENTS

- 2 tablespoons unsalted butter
- 1/3 cup sugar
- ¾ cup cornmeal
- ½ tablespoon salt
- 2 tablespoons baking powder
- 1 cup non-fat buttermilk
- 1 egg
- 1 cup flour

DIRECTIONS

1. Mix all ingredients together in a bowl.
2. Wait for 5 to 10 minutes.

3. Line a non-stick tin with muffin papers.

4. Divide the batter into twelve muffins and bake at 330 F for 12-15 minutes.

Nutritional Facts

Amount Per Serving

Calories 105	Calories from Fat 15
	% Daily Value
Total Fat 2g	3%
Saturated Fat 1g	4%
Monounsaturated Fat 1g	
Trans Fat 0g	
Cholesterol 20mg	7%
Sodium 228mg	9%
Total Carbohydrates 20g	7%
Dietary Fiber 1g	3%
Sugars 6g	
Protein 3g	
Vitamin A 1%	Vitamin C 0%
Calcium 7%	Iron 5%
Vitamin K 0 mcg	Potassium 39 mg
Magnesium 12 mg	

DATE NUT QUICKBREAD

Serves: **8**
Prep Time: **15** minutes
Cook Time: **65** minutes
Total Time: **80** minutes

INGREDIENTS

- ½ cup chopped dates
- 2 tablespoons molasses
- ¼ cup wheat germ
- ¼ low-fat buttermilk
- ½ unsweetened applesauce
- ½ tablespoon pure vanilla extract
- 3 large egg whites
- ½ cup boiling water
- 1 egg yolk
- 1 ¼ cup flour
- ¼ tablespoon salt
- 2 tablespoon baking powder
- ½ tablespoon baking soda
- 1 ½ tablespoon chopped pecans
- 2 tablespoons canola oil

- ½ sweet stevia
- ¾ cup wheat flour

DIRECTIONS

1. Preheat oven to 350 F.
2. Line a 1 ½ quart glass Pyrex oblong loaf pan with foil.
3. Place the dates in a bowl and cover the boiling water.
4. Wait for about 10-15 minutes.
5. Whisk the egg yolk until smooth.
6. Add canola oil, applesauce, sweet stevia, vanilla extract and whisk together.
7. In a bowl whisk the egg whites until they begin to be white.
8. Place the flour, wheat flour, baking soda, cinnamon, baking powder, wheat germ in a sifter and sift into a bowl.
9. Fold the mixture creamed together with the flour mixture.
10. Add butter and fold until smooth.
11. Pour the batter into the lined Pyrex dish.
12. Place the loaf pan in the preheated oven.

Nutritional Facts

Amount Per Serving

Calories 248	Calories from Fat 59
	% Daily Value
Total Fat 7g	11%
Saturated Fat 1g	4%
Monounsaturated Fat 4g	
Trans Fat 0g	
Cholesterol 27mg	9%
Sodium 304mg	13%
Total Carbohydrates 43g	14%
Dietary Fiber 4g	17%
Sugars 13g	
Protein 8g	
Vitamin A 1%	Vitamin C 1%
Calcium 12%	Iron 12%
Vitamin K 2 mcg	Potassium 318 mg
Magnesium 56 mg	

GINGERBREAD

Serves: *8*
Prep Time: *15*   minutes
Cook Time: *65*   minutes
Total Time: *80*   minutes

INGREDIENTS

- 3 large egg whites
- ½ tablespoon pure vanilla
- 3 tablespoons molasses
- 1 egg yolk
- 2 tablespoons canola oil
- ¾ cup wheat flour
- ¼ tablespoon salt
- 2 ½ tablespoon baking powder
- ½ cup Sweet Stevia
- ½ tablespoon soda
- ½ cup unsweetened applesauce
- 1 tablespoon cinnamon
- 2 tablespoons ginger
- ¼ wheat germ
- ½ cup low-fat buttermilk
- ½ cup canned pumpkin

- 1 ¼ cup flour

DIRECTIONS

1. Preheat oven to 350 F.
2. Line a 1 ½ quart glass Pyrex loaf pan with foil.
3. Whisk the egg yolk until smooth and add canola oil and whisk them.
4. Add Applesauce, canned pumpkin, sweet stevia and vanilla extract and whisk them.
5. Whisk the egg whites until they begin to be white.
6. Add flour, wheat flour, cinnamon, baking soda, baking powder, wheat germ and ginger in a sifter and sift in a bowl.
7. Fold the creamed mixture with the flour mixture and add buttermilk.
8. When the mixture is blended add egg whites and fold together.
9. Pour the batter into the lined Pyrex dish.
10. Bake for 55 minutes.

Nutritional Facts

Amount Per Serving

Calories 178	Calories from Fat 18
	% Daily Value
Total Fat 2g	3%
Saturated Fat 0g	2%
Monounsaturated Fat 1g	
Trans Fat 0g	
Cholesterol 27mg	9%
Sodium 347mg	14%
Total Carbohydrates 35g	11%
Dietary Fiber 3g	13%
Sugars 6g	
Protein 7g	
Vitamin A 49%	Vitamin C 2%
Calcium 11%	Iron 13%
Vitamin K 3 mcg	Potassium 268 mg
Magnesium 48 mg	

GLUTEN FREE GINGERBREAD

Serves: **8**
Prep Time: **15** minutes
Cook Time: **65** minutes
Total Time: **80** minutes

INGREDIENTS

- 3 molasses
- 3 egg whites
- 1 egg yolk
- 1 ¼ cup gluten free flour
- ¾ gluten free grain flour
- ¼ salt
- 2 tablespoons canola oil
- 1 tablespoon cinnamon
- 3 tablespoons ginger
- ½ unsweetened applesauce
- ½ tablespoon vanilla extract
- ½ non-fat buttermilk
- ½ canned pumpkin
- ½ cup sweet stevia
- 2 ½ tablespoons baking powder
- ¼ tablespoon baking soda

DIRECTIONS

1. Preheat oven to 350 F.
2. Line a 1 ½ quart glass Pyrex loaf pan with foil.
3. In a bowl whisk the egg yolk until smooth.
4. Add oil and whisk them until smooth
5. Add pumpkin, applesauce, stevia and vanilla extract and whisk together.
6. In another bowl, whisk the egg whites.
7. Add gluten free flour, salt, gluten free grain flour, baking powder, baking soda, ginger and cinnamon in a sifter and sift them into a bowl.
8. Fold the creamed mixture with the flour mixture.
9. When the mixture is blended, add the egg whites and fold together, also add buttermilk.
10. Pour the batter into the lined Pyrex dish and place the loaf pan in the oven.
11. Bake for 50-55 minutes.

Nutritional Facts

Calories 225	Calories from Fat 31
	% Daily Value
Total Fat 3g	6%
Saturated Fat <1g	2%
Monounsaturated Fat 1g	
Trans Fat 0g	
Cholesterol 29mg	9%
Sodium 317mg	13%
Total Carbohydrates 39g	14%
Dietary Fiber 3g	11%
Sugars 7g	
Protein 4g	
Vitamin A 47%	Vitamin C 1%
Calcium 10%	Iron 8%
Vitamin K 3 mcg	Potassium 310 mg
Magnesium 44 mg	

LEMON POPPYSEED MUFFINS

Serves: **6**
Prep Time: **15**   minutes
Cook Time: **25**   minutes
Total Time: **40**   minutes

INGREDIENTS

- 1 large egg
- ¼ tablespoon baking soda
- ½ cup wheat flour
- 2 tablespoon wheat germ
- 1 ½ tablespoon baking powder
- ¼ salt
- 1/3 cup low-fat buttermilk
- 3 tablespoons non-fat yogurt
- 2 tablespoons canola oil
- ¼ cup lemon juice
- ½ tablespoon vanilla extract
- 2 tablespoons poppy seeds
- 1 ½ tablespoon lemon zest
- ½ cup sweet stevia
- 1 cup white flour

DIRECTIONS

1. Preheat oven to 375 F.
2. Separate the egg white and the egg yolk and place the egg yolk in a bowl.
3. Add canola oil in the bowl and whisk together.
4. Add vanilla extract, yogurt, sweet stevia, lemon zest, poppy seeds and lemon juice and whisk them.
5. Add the flour, wheat flour, salt, baking soda, baking powder, wheat germ in a sifter and sift into a bowl.
6. Fold the flour mixture with the creamed mixture.
7. Add buttermilk and as the mixture is blended, stop.
8. Whisk the egg white until white.
9. Line a standard size muffin tin with 6 muffin papers and fill each muffin paper with an equal amount of batter.
10. Bake for 20 minutes.

Nutritional Facts

Amount Per Serving

Calories 169	Calories from Fat 31

	% Daily Value
Total Fat 4g	6%
Saturated Fat 1g	4%
Monounsaturated Fat 1g	
Trans Fat 0g	
Cholesterol 38mg	12%
Sodium 273mg	11%
Total Carbohydrates 28g	9%
Dietary Fiber 3g	11%
Sugars 2g	
Protein 6g	
Vitamin A 1%	Vitamin C 11%
Calcium 14%	Iron 11%
Vitamin K 1 mcg	Potassium 188 mg
Magnesium 39 mg	

ORANGE ALMOND MUFFINS

Serves: **6**
Prep Time: **5**   minutes
Cook Time: **40**   minutes
Total Time: **45**   minutes

INGREDIENTS

- 1 egg separated
- 1/3 cup orange juice
- 2 tablespoons canola oil
- ¼ baking soda
- ½ cup almonds
- ¼ cup low-fat buttermilk
- 1 cup wheat flour
- ¼ tablespoon salt
- 1 tablespoon baking powder
- 2 tablespoons wheat germ
- 1 tablespoon orange zest
- ½ cup sweet stevia
- 2 tablespoons brown sugar
- 3 tablespoons non-fat yogurt
- 1 ½ almond extract

DIRECTIONS

1. Preheat oven to 375 F.
2. Beat the egg yolk and cream together with canola oil.
3. Add sweet stevia and whisk until smooth and then add almond extract and yogurt.
4. Add the purpose flour, wheat flour, salt, baking soda and baking powder in a sifter and sift into a bowl.
5. Add wheat germ, orange zest and ¼ cup of almonds.
6. Fold the flour mixture together with the creamed mixture.
7. When is blended whisk the egg white until white.
8. Add buttermilk and orange juice and blend them.
9. Line a standard size muffin tin with 6 muffin papers and fill each muffin paper with an equal amount of batter.
10. Sprinkle the top with brown sugar.
11. Bake for 20 minutes.

Nutritional Facts

Amount Per Serving

Calories 232	Calories from Fat 71

	% Daily Value
Total Fat 8g	13%
Saturated Fat 1g	5%
Monounsaturated Fat 5g	
Trans Fat 0g	
Cholesterol 35mg	12%
Sodium 258mg	11%
Total Carbohydrates 29g	10%
Dietary Fiber 3g	14%
Sugars 4g	
Protein 9g	
Vitamin A 1%	Vitamin C 12%
Calcium 11%	Iron 12%
Vitamin K 1 mcg	Potassium 241 mg
Magnesium 65 mg	

ORANGE FRENCH TOAST

Serves: *8*
Prep Time: *5*   minutes
Cook Time: *60*   minutes
Total Time: *65*   minutes

INGREDIENTS

- 1 tablespoon stevia
- ¼ orange juice
- ¼ orange peel
- 3 ounces egg substitute
- 1 tablespoon 2% milk
- 1 ½ tablespoon honey
- ¼ tablespoon vanilla extract
- 3 tablespoons unsalted butter
- 3 tablespoons orange liqueur
- 4 slices bread

DIRECTIONS

1. Place the egg substitute, milk, vanilla extract, stevia, orange juice and orange peel in a mixing bowl.

2. Heat a non-stick griddle over high heat.

3. When the griddle is hot enough place 4 slices of bread into the batter.

4. Turn the bread until it is well coated and slightly soaked.

5. Place the 4 slices of soaked bread on the griddle and cook for 5 minutes(cook on each side).

6. Serve one tablespoon of orange honey for every slice of French toast.

Nutritional Facts

Amount Per Serving

Calories 340	Calories from Fat 51
	% Daily Value
Total Fat 6g	9%
Saturated Fat 2g	8%
Monounsaturated Fat 2g	
Trans Fat 0g	
Cholesterol 1mg	0%
Sodium 525mg	22%
Total Carbohydrates 59g	20%
Dietary Fiber 2g	7%
Sugars 24g	

Protein 11g

Vitamin A 13%	Vitamin C 27%
Calcium 5%	Iron 17%
Vitamin K 4 mcg	Potassium 248 mg
Magnesium 28 mg	

PECAN PEACH MUFFINS

Serves: **6**
Prep Time: **15**   minutes
Cook Time: **30**   minutes
Total Time: **45**   minutes

INGREDIENTS

- 3 tablespoons non-fat buttermilk
- 2 tablespoons brown sugar
- ¼ cup chopped pecans
- 1 large egg
- ¼ tablespoon baking soda
- ½ nutmeg
- 2 tablespoons wheat germ
- 1 cup flour
- ½ wheat flour
- ½ tablespoon vanilla extract
- ½ sweet stevia
- 2 ½ tablespoons honey
- ¼ salt
- 1 ½ tablespoon baking powder
- 2 tablespoons canola oil
- 8-ounces peaches

DIRECTIONS

1. Preheat oven to 375 F.
2. Cream together the egg yolk and canola oil.
3. Add peaches and mash them into the mixture.
4. Add vanilla extract, honey and stevia and blend well.
5. Sift the flour, wheat flour, salt, baking soda, baking powder, wheat germ and nutmeg in sifter and sift into a bowl.
6. Fold the creamed mixture together with the flour mixture.
7. Whisk the egg white until is white.
8. Fold in the buttermilk and when the dough is blended stop.
9. Line a standard size tin with 6 muffin papers.
10. Fill each muffin paper with an equal amount of batter.
11. Mix with brown sugar and then sprinkle over the top of muffins.
12. Bake for 25 minutes.

Nutritional Facts

Amount Per Serving

Calories 222	Calories from Fat 54
	% Daily Value
Total Fat 6g	10%
Saturated Fat 1g	4%
Monounsaturated Fat 3g	
Trans Fat 0g	
Cholesterol 37mg	12%
Sodium 246mg	10%
Total Carbohydrates 37g	12%
Dietary Fiber 3g	13%
Sugars 11g	
Protein 5g	
Vitamin A 3%	Vitamin C 4%
Calcium 7%	Iron 11%
Vitamin K 3 mcg	Potassium 201 mg
Magnesium 32 mg	

PECAN SWEET POTATO BREAD

Serves: **8**
Prep Time: **5**   minutes
Cook Time: **50**   minutes
Total Time: **55**   minutes

INGREDIENTS

- 1 8-ounce yam
- ¼ tablespoon salt
- 2 tablespoons baking powder
- ½ cinnamon
- 3 tablespoons wheat germ
- ½ tablespoon baking soda
- ¼ cup non-fat buttermilk
- 2 tablespoons brown sugar
- ½ sweet stevia
- 1 ½ tablespoon vanilla extract
- ½ cup chopped pecans
- 3 egg whites
- 1 ¼ cup flour
- 1 large egg yolk
- 2 tablespoons canola oil
- ¾ cup wheat flour

DIRECTIONS

1. Preheat oven to 375 F.
2. Line a 1 ½ quart glass Pyrex loaf pan with oil.
3. Whisk the egg yolk until smooth and then add canola oil.
4. Add sweet stevia, vanilla extract and mashed yams and whisk.
5. Fold the chopped pecans.
6. In another bowl whisk the egg whites until they are white.
7. Add the flour, wheat flour, baking soda, baking powder, salt, wheat germ and cinnamon in a sifter and sift into a bowl.
8. Fold the creamed mixture together with the flour mixture.
9. Add buttermilk and fold until smooth.
10. When the mixture is blended add egg whites and fold together.
11. Pour the batter into the lined Pyrex dish.
12. Sprinkled brown sugar over the top of the bread.
13. Bake for 50 minutes.

Nutritional Facts

Amount Per Serving

Calories 225	Calories from Fat 57
	% Daily Value
Total Fat 7g	10%
Saturated Fat 1g	4%
Monounsaturated Fat 4g	
Trans Fat 0g	
Cholesterol 25mg	9%
Sodium 303mg	13%
Total Carbohydrates 35g	12%
Dietary Fiber 4g	16%
Sugars 2g	
Protein 7g	
Vitamin A 2%	Vitamin C 8%
Calcium 10%	Iron 11%
Vitamin K 2 mcg	Potassium 377 mg
Magnesium 43 mg	

PUMPKIN BREAD

Serves: *8*
Prep Time: *15*   minutes
Cook Time: *85*   minutes
Total Time: *100*   minutes

INGREDIENTS

- 3 tablespoons brown sugar
- 1 egg yolk
- 2 tablespoons canola oil
- ½ cup dried pumpkin seeds
- ½ tablespoon cinnamon
- ¼ tablespoon nutmeg
- ¼ tablespoon allspice
- 1 ¼ white flour
- ¼ ground cloves
- ¼ wheat germ
- 1/3 non-fat buttermilk
- 1 cup canned pumpkin
- 3 egg whites
- 2/3 cup sweet stevia
- ½ tablespoon vanilla extract
- ¾ cup wheat flour

- ¼ tablespoons salt
- 3 tablespoons baking powder
- ½ tablespoon baking soda

DIRECTIONS

1. Preheat oven to 350 F.
2. Line a 1 ½ quart glass Pyrex loaf pan with foil.
3. Whisk the egg yolk until smooth and add reduced fat spread and whisk them until smooth.
4. Whisk the canned pumpkin into the mixture and add vanilla extract, stevia and whisk together.
5. In a bowl whisk the egg whites until they are white.
6. Place the wheat flour, flour, salt, baking soda, baking powder, nutmeg, cinnamon, cloves and wheat germ in a sifter and sift into a bowl.
7. Fold the creamed mixture together with the flour mixture.
8. When the mixture is well blended add the egg whites and fold together until smooth.
9. Add the buttermilk and fold.
10. Pour the batter into the lined Pyrex and sprinkle the brown sugar over the top.

11. Bake for 70-80 minutes.

Nutritional Facts

Amount Per Serving	
Calories 237	Calories from Fat 68
	% Daily Value
Total Fat 8g	12%
Saturated Fat 2g	8%
Monounsaturated Fat 3g	
Trans Fat 0g	
Cholesterol 27mg	9%
Sodium 377mg	16%
Total Carbohydrates 32g	11%
Dietary Fiber 4g	16%
Sugars 3g	
Protein 11g	
Vitamin A 97%	Vitamin C 3%
Calcium 11%	Iron 24%
Vitamin K 12 mcg	Potassium 318 mg
Magnesium 112 mg	

ZUCCHINI BREAD

Serves: **8**
Prep Time: **15**   minutes
Cook Time: **55**   minutes
Total Time: **70**   minutes

INGREDIENTS

- ½ cup non-fat buttermilk
- 2 cups zucchini
- ¼ cup raisins
- ¼ cup dried pumpkin seeds
- ¾ cup wheat flout
- ¼ salt
- 3 egg whites
- 1 ¼ white flour
- 3 tablespoons baking powder
- ½ tablespoons baking soda
- 2 ½ tablespoons brown sugar
- ¼ cinnamon
- 1 egg yolk
- 1 tablespoon canola oil
- 3 tablespoons non-fat yogurt
- ½ tablespoons vanilla extract

- ½ cinnamon
- ¼ ground nutmeg
- ¼ oatmeal
- 2/3 cup sweet stevia

DIRECTIONS

1. Preheat oven to 350 F.
2. Line a 1 ½ quart glass Pyrex loaf pan with foil.
3. Take a skillet and turn heat on high and add the pumpkin seeds.
4. Cook while stirring until the seeds are done.
5. Add the toasted seeds in a bowl and add the two teaspoons of brown sugar and cinnamon and stir.
6. Whisk the egg yolk and add canola oil and whisk together until smooth.
7. Add sweet stevia, vanilla extract and yogurt and whisk them.
8. In a bowl whisk egg whites until they are white.
9. Fold the creamed mixture together with the flour mixture and add zucchini and raisins.
10. As the zucchini is blended add buttermilk and fold until smooth.

11. When mixture is blended add egg whites and fold together.

12. Pour the batter into the lined Pyrex and sprinkle the pumpkin seed over the top.

13. Bake for 55-60 minutes.

Nutritional Facts

Amount Per Serving	
Calories 220	Calories from Fat 45
	% Daily Value
Total Fat 5g	8%
Saturated Fat 1g	6%
Monounsaturated Fat 2g	
Trans Fat 0g	
Cholesterol 28mg	9%
Sodium 322mg	13%
Total Carbohydrates 38g	12%
Dietary Fiber 3g	12%
Sugars 7g	
Protein 10g	
Vitamin A 3%	Vitamin C 10%
Calcium 13%	Iron 16%
Vitamin K 6 mcg	Potassium 335 mg
Magnesium 73 mg	

PANCAKES

PAN BAKED APPLE PANCAKE

Serves: **4**
Prep Time: **5**   minutes
Cook Time: **30** minutes
Total Time: **35** minutes

INGREDIENTS

- 3 egg whites
- 2 lbs. apples
- 2 ½ tablespoons butter
- ¾ white flour
- ¼ salt
- 3 tablespoons butter
- ½ cup stevia
- 1 large egg yolk
- 2 tablespoons stevia
- ¾ non-fat buttermilk
- ¼ cup water

DIRECTIONS

1. Preheat oven to 425 F.
2. In an iron skillet heat the butter, stevia and water.
3. Cook the apples for 15 minutes.
4. Stir them every 2 minutes.
5. The mixture will turn a golden brown caramel color.
6. Meanwhile place the egg whites, egg yolk, salt, flour, buttermilk and add stevia in the blended.
7. Blend until smooth.
8. Pour the flour mixture over the apples when they are caramelized.
9. Put the pan in the oven.
10. Bake for 15-20 minutes.

Nutritional Facts

Amount Per Serving

Calories 208	Calories from Fat 50
	% Daily Value
Total Fat 6g	9%
Saturated Fat 3g	16%
Monounsaturated Fat 2g	
Trans Fat 0g	
Cholesterol 64mg	21%
Sodium 235mg	10%

Total Carbohydrates 31g	10%
Dietary Fiber 2g	10%
Sugars 11g	
Protein 8g	

Vitamin A 4%	Vitamin C 6%
Calcium 7%	Iron 7%
Vitamin K 1 mcg	Potassium 218 mg
Magnesium 19 mg	

BLUEBERRY BLUE CORNMEAL PANCAKES

Serves: **2**
Prep Time: **5**   minutes
Cook Time: **35** minutes
Total Time: **40** minutes

INGREDIENTS

- ½ cup blue cornmeal
- 2 ½ tablespoons stevia
- 2 tablespoons blueberries
- 3 tablespoons butter
- ¼ egg substitute
- 1 ½ tablespoon baking powder
- ¼ tablespoon salt
- 2/3 cup non-fat buttermilk
- 1 tablespoon vanilla extract
- ¼ cup wheat flour
- 1 tablespoon maple syrup

DIRECTIONS

1. Add the cornmeal, stevia, baking powder, wheat flour and salt in a sifter and sift them.

2. Add the egg substitute, buttermilk and vanilla extract and whisk them.

3. Heat a non-stick griddle.

4. Let the batter stand in the griddle while is heating and stir.

5. When the griddle is hot enough reduce the heat and add ¼ cup of batter for each pancake.

6. When pancakes are cooked add a tablespoon of blueberries over each one.

7. Cook for another 2-3 minutes.

8. Turn pancake and cook for 1-2 minutes until they are brown.

Nutritional Facts

Amount Per Serving	
Calories 365	Calories from Fat 69
	% Daily Value
Total Fat 8g	12%
Saturated Fat 2g	10%
Monounsaturated Fat 2.5g	
Trans Fat 0g	

Cholesterol 4mg	1%
Sodium 325mg	13%
Total Carbohydrates 62g	21%
Dietary Fiber 6g	23%
Sugars 19g	
Protein 13g	
Vitamin A 12%	Vitamin C 6%
Calcium 20%	Iron 16%
Vitamin K 7 mcg	Potassium 496 mg
Magnesium 91 mg	

BUCKWHEAT PANCAKES

Serves: **2**
Prep Time: **5**   minutes
Cook Time: **25**   minutes
Total Time: **30**   minutes

INGREDIENTS

- 1 egg yolk
- ¼ champagne
- 1/3 cup buckwheat flour
- 1/3 cup flour
- 1/8 salt
- 2 egg whites
- 2 tablespoons butter
- 2 tablespoons maple syrup
- 3 tablespoons milk

DIRECTIONS

1. Whisk the egg yolk with the champagne and milk until well blended.
2. Slowly blend in the flour, buckwheat flour and salt until smooth.

3. Whisk the egg whites until they are white.

4. Fold the egg whites into the buckwheat batter.

5. Heat a griddle and melt one teaspoon of the butter on the griddle and add the batter in 1/3 cup scoops.

6. Cook the pancakes on each side for 2 minutes.

Nutritional Facts

Amount Per Serving

Calories 320	Calories from Fat 81
	% Daily Value
Total Fat 9g	14%
Saturated Fat 5g	24%
Monounsaturated Fat 3g	
Trans Fat 0g	
Cholesterol 121mg	40%
Sodium 484mg	20%
Total Carbohydrates 44g	15%
Dietary Fiber 3g	10%
Sugars 14g	
Protein 10g	
Vitamin A 6%	Vitamin C 0%
Calcium 13%	Iron 13%
Vitamin K 2 mcg	Potassium 294 mg
Magnesium 68 mg	

BUTTERMILK PANCAKES

Serves: 2
Prep Time: 5   minutes
Cook Time: 15   minutes
Total Time: 20   minutes

INGREDIENTS

- 1 egg
- 1 tablespoon vanilla extract
- 2/3 cup white flour
- 2 tablespoon butter
- 2 tablespoon maple syrup
- 2/3 cup non-fat buttermilk
- 1 tablespoon baking powder
- 1 ½ tablespoons stevia

DIRECTIONS

1. Sift stevia, flour and baking powder in a bowl.
2. Add buttermilk, vanilla extract, egg and blend them.
3. Heat a griddle over high and let the batter stand for 2 minutes.

4. Stir from time to time.

5. When griddle is hot enough, reduce heat and add ¼ cup of batter.

6. Cook each pancake for 2-3 minutes on each side.

Nutritional Facts

Amount Per Serving

Calories 325	Calories from Fat 74
	% Daily Value
Total Fat 8g	13%
Saturated Fat 2g	12%
Monounsaturated Fat 3g	
Trans Fat 0g	
Cholesterol 109mg	36%
Sodium 406mg	17%
Total Carbohydrates 51g	17%
Dietary Fiber 1g	5%
Sugars 12g	
Protein 11g	
Vitamin A 20%	Vitamin C 2%
Calcium 28%	Iron 16%
Vitamin K 7 mcg	Potassium 277 mg
Magnesium 27 mg	

EASY GRANOLA

Serves: **6**
Prep Time: **15**   minutes
Cook Time: **70**   minutes
Total Time: **85**   minutes

INGREDIENTS

- 2/3 quinoa
- ¼ sliced almonds
- ¼ walnuts
- 3 quarts water
- 3 tablespoons maple syrup
- ¼ raisins
- ¼ cranberries
- ½ unsweetened applesauce
- ½ tablespoon cinnamon
- 1 1/3 oats
- ½ nutmeg
- 1/8 salt

DIRECTIONS

1. Preheat oven to 300 F.
2. Add the water in a large sauce pan.

3. When the water is boiling add quinoa and oats.

4. Reduce the heat and cook for 10-15 minutes.

5. Drain with cold water.

6. Put the drained oats and quinoa in a bowl.

7. Add over almonds, applesauce, walnuts, cinnamon, salt, nutmeg, raisins, maple syrup and cranberries.

8. Place on a large cookie sheet lined with aluminum and spread as flat as possible.

9. Bake for 40-50 minutes and stir with a fork.

Nutritional Facts

Amount Per Serving		
Calories 237	Calories from Fat 56	
	% Daily Value	
Total Fat 7g		10%
Saturated Fat 1g		4%
Monounsaturated Fat 2g		
Trans Fat 0g		
Cholesterol 0mg		0%
Sodium 39mg		2%
Total Carbohydrates 40g		13%

Dietary Fiber 5g		20%
Sugars 10g		
Protein 8g		
Vitamin A 0%	Vitamin C 6%	
Calcium 4%	Iron 13%	
Vitamin K 0 mcg	Potassium 286 mg	
Magnesium 92 mg		

WHOLE GRAIN PANCAKES

Serves: 2
Prep Time: 5   minutes
Cook Time: 25   minutes
Total Time: 30   minutes

INGREDIENTS

- 1 tablespoon stevia
- 6 tablespoons oatmeal
- 1 tablespoon baking powder
- 6 tablespoons white flour
- 1 cup non-fat buttermilk
- 2 tablespoons maple syrup
- 1/8 tablespoon salt
- 6 tablespoons wheat flour
- 1 large egg
- 2 egg whites
- 2 tablespoons cornmeal
- 3 tablespoons butter

DIRECTIONS

1. Sift the flour, wheat flour, corn meal, baking powder and salt into a bowl and fold in the oatmeal.

2. Add egg substitute, buttermilk and blend until mixture is smooth.

3. Heat a griddle over high heat and let the batter stand for 2 minutes.

4. Stir from time to time.

5. When the griddle is hot enough, reduce heat and place ¼ cup of batter.

6. Cook each pancake for 2-3 minutes on each side.

7. Serve one tablespoon of maple syrup for every pancake.

Nutritional Facts

Amount Per Serving	
Calories 435	Calories from Fat 70
	% Daily Value
Total Fat 8g	12%
Saturated Fat 2g	12%
Monounsaturated Fat 3g	
Trans Fat 0g	
Cholesterol 105mg	36%
Sodium 469mg	20%

Total Carbohydrates 76g		25%
Dietary Fiber 6g		24%
Sugars 19g		
Protein 17g		
Vitamin A 18%	Vitamin C 2%	
Calcium 34%	Iron 20%	
Vitamin K 4 mcg	Potassium 482 mg	
Magnesium 87 mg		

JEAN'S FRENCH TOAST

Serves: **2**
Prep Time: **10**   minutes
Cook Time: **25**   minutes
Total Time: **35**   minutes

INGREDIENTS

- 6 tablespoons 2% milk
- 6 tablespoons egg substitute
- 3 tablespoons stevia
- 2 tablespoons butter
- ¼ tablespoon nutmeg
- ½ tablespoon vanilla extract
- 1/8 salt
- 4 1 ounce slices bread
- 2 tablespoons maple syrup

DIRECTIONS

1. Place the milk, stevia, egg substitute, nutmeg, salt and vanilla extract in a bowl and whisk until well blended.
2. Heat a griddle over high heat.

3. When the griddle is hot enough, reduce the heat and place 4 slices of bread into the batter.

4. Dunk and turn the bread until it is well coated.

5. Place the 4 slices of soaked bread in the griddle.

6. Cook for 3 minutes on each side.

7. Top with one teaspoon of butter on each piece of toast and serve with one tablespoon of maple syrup for each slice of French toast.

Nutritional Facts

Amount Per Serving	
Calories 348	Calories from Fat 65
	% Daily Value
Total Fat 7g	11%
Saturated Fat 2g	11%
Monounsaturated Fat 2g	
Trans Fat 0g	
Cholesterol 4mg	1%
Sodium 721mg	30%
Total Carbohydrates 56g	18%
Dietary Fiber 2g	6%
Sugars 19g	

Protein 15g

Vitamin A 15%	Vitamin C 0%
Calcium 12%	Iron 20%
Vitamin K 4 mcg	Potassium 355 mg
Magnesium 30 mg	

CLASSIC SHREDDED HASH BROWNS

Serves: 2
Prep Time: 5   minutes
Cook Time: 15   minutes
Total Time: 20   minutes

INGREDIENTS

- 3 tablespoons butter
- 1/8 salt
- 8 ounces gold potatoes (shredded)
- 1/8 black pepper

DIRECTIONS

1. Shred the potatoes and place them in a strainer.
2. Use a rubber spatula and press the excess water out of them.
3. Place the potatoes on a paper towel and pat as dry as possible.
4. Put the potatoes in a bowl and add salt and pepper.
5. Place the butter on a griddle over high heat.

6. When the butter is melted, add the potatoes.

7. Toss well on the griddle for 5 minutes and then gather the potatoes.

8. Cook the potatoes slowly to medium heat.

9. Cook on each side for 3 minutes.

Nutritional Facts

Amount Per Serving	
Calories 115	Calories from Fat 36
	% Daily Value
Total Fat 4g	6%
Saturated Fat 2g	10%
Monounsaturated Fat 1g	
Trans Fat 0g	
Cholesterol 10mg	3%
Sodium 153mg	6%
Total Carbohydrates 19g	8%
Dietary Fiber 2g	8%
Sugars 1g	
Protein 2g	
Vitamin A 2%	Vitamin C 16%
Calcium 0%	Iron 4%
Vitamin K 3 mcg	Potassium 517 mg
Magnesium 22 mg	

HEALTHY TOASTED OATMEAL

Serves: **1**
Prep Time: **5**   minutes
Cook Time: **10**   minutes
Total Time: **15**   minutes

INGREDIENTS

- 2 tablespoons butter
- 1/8 tablespoon salt
- ½ cup oats
- 1 ½ tablespoon brown sugar
- ½ cup water
- ½ cup 2% milk

DIRECTIONS

1. Place a steel skillet over high heat.
2. Add the oatmeal and cook for 3-4 minutes.
3. Stir frequently so that the oatmeal won't burn.
4. Reduce the heat to medium.
5. Oatmeal should have a golden brown color.

6. Remove the pan from the heat and add water.

7. Put the pan back over low heat and add milk, sugar and salt.

8. Cook for 5 more minutes.

Nutritional Facts

Amount Per Serving	
Calories 264	Calories from Fat 58
	% Daily Value
Total Fat 7g	10%
Saturated Fat 2g	12%
Monounsaturated Fat 2g	
Trans Fat 0g	
Cholesterol 11mg	3%
Sodium 246mg	10%
Total Carbohydrates 40g	13%
Dietary Fiber 4g	16%
Sugars 14g	
Protein 12g	
Vitamin A 5%	Vitamin C 2%
Calcium 20%	Iron 11%
Vitamin K 3 mcg	Potassium 82 mg
Magnesium 392 mg	

POLENTA AND EGGS

Serves: **1**
Prep Time: **5**   minutes
Cook Time: **15** minutes
Total Time: **20** minutes

INGREDIENTS

- 1/8 salt
- 1 large egg
- 1 cup water
- ¼ cup cornmeal
- 1 tablespoon Parmigiano-Reggiano

DIRECTIONS

1. Preheat the oven to 375 F.
2. Place the water in a small sauce pan over high heat.
3. Whisk in the polenta.
4. Add salt and pepper to the pan.
5. Reduce the heat to medium while polenta is simmering and continue to whisk.

6. Polenta should be ready in 5 minutes.

7. Pour the polenta into a dish.

8. Crack the egg and pour it in the middle of the polenta.

9. Put the dish in the oven and bake for 5 minutes.

10. Sprinkle with parmesan over the top.

11. Cook for another 3 minutes.

Nutritional Facts

Amount Per Serving	
Calories 190	Calories from Fat 58
	% Daily Value
Total Fat 7g	10%
Saturated Fat 2g	10%
Monounsaturated Fat 2g	
Trans Fat 0g	
Cholesterol 42mg	14%
Sodium 400mg	17%
Total Carbohydrates 24g	8%
Dietary Fiber 2g	9%
Sugars 1g	
Protein 10g	
Vitamin A 6%	Vitamin C 0%
Calcium 5%	Iron 11%
Vitamin K 1 mcg	Potassium 156 mg
Magnesium 48 mg	

SCRAMBLED EGGS

Serves: **2**
Prep Time: **5**   minutes
Cook Time: **20**   minutes
Total Time: **25**   minutes

INGREDIENTS

- 8 ounces mushrooms
- 1/8 tablespoon black pepper
- 3 egg whites
- 3 tablespoons water
- 1/8 tablespoon salt
- 1 egg yolk
- 2 tablespoons butter

DIRECTIONS

1. Place the egg yolk, egg whites, salt and water in a bowl and whisk until frothy.
2. Melt the butter in a small skillet pan over high heat.
3. Sauté the mushrooms until browned.
4. Cook the mushrooms until they are caramel brown.

5. Add egg mixture and stir the eggs.

6. Add black pepper and serve.

Nutritional Facts

Amount Per Serving

Calories 99	Calories from Fat 45
	% Daily Value
Total Fat 5g	7%
Saturated Fat 2g	11%
Monounsaturated Fat 2g	
Trans Fat 0g	
Cholesterol 110mg	37%
Sodium 383mg	16%
Total Carbohydrates 5g	1%
Dietary Fiber 1g	4%
Sugars 2g	
Protein 10g	
Vitamin A 4%	Vitamin C 4%
Calcium 2%	Iron 5%
Vitamin K 0 mcg	Potassium 447 mg
Magnesium 13 mg	

SHREDDED SWEET POTATO HASH BROWNS

Serves: **2**
Prep Time: **10**   minutes
Cook Time: **25**   minutes
Total Time: **35**   minutes

INGREDIENTS

- 8 ounces sweet potatoes
- 3 tablespoons butter
- 1 ½ tablespoon dried sage
- 1/8 tablespoon black pepper
- 1/8 tablespoon salt

DIRECTIONS

1. Shred the potatoes and place them in a strainer.
2. Use a rubber spatula and press the excess water.
3. Place the potatoes on a paper towel and pat as dry as possible.
4. Put the potatoes in a bowl and add sage, salt and pepper.
5. Place the butter in a skillet over high heat.

6. When the butter is melted add the potatoes.

7. Toss well for 5 minutes and gather them together into two piles.

8. Cook the potatoes slowly.

9. Cook on each side for 3 minutes.

Nutritional Facts

Amount Per Serving	
Calories 171	Calories from Fat 37
	% Daily Value
Total Fat 4g	6%
Saturated Fat 2g	10%
Monounsaturated Fat 1g	
Trans Fat 0g	
Cholesterol 10mg	3%
Sodium 156mg	6%
Total Carbohydrates 33g	12%
Dietary Fiber 5g	17%
Sugars 1g	
Protein 2g	
Vitamin A 7%	Vitamin C 32%
Calcium 1%	Iron 5%
Vitamin K 9 mcg	Potassium 930 mg
Magnesium 29 mg	

STRAWBERRY BANANA SMOOTHIE

Serves: **1**
Prep Time: **5**   minutes
Cook Time: **10** minutes
Total Time: **15** minutes

INGREDIENTS

- ¼ cup non-fat yogurt
- ½ banana
- 1 cup strawberries
- ½ cup mango juice

DIRECTIONS

1. **Place the strawberries, mango juice, yogurt and banana in a blender.**
2. **Blend until smooth.**

Nutritional Facts

Amount Per Serving	
Calories 233	Calories from Fat 0
	% Daily Value
Total Fat 1g	1%
Saturated Fat 0g	1%

Monounsaturated Fat 0g	
Trans Fat 0g	
Cholesterol 33mg	1%
Sodium 103mg	4%
Total Carbohydrates 51g	17%
Dietary Fiber 5g	20%
Sugars 40g	
Protein 9g	
Vitamin A 19%	Vitamin C 191%
Calcium 29%	Iron 7%
Vitamin K 5 mcg	Potassium 786 mg
Magnesium 65 mg	

TORTILLA WITH YAMS

Serves: *8*
Prep Time: *15*   minutes
Cook Time: *45*   minutes
Total Time: *60*   minutes

INGREDIENTS

- 8 ounces yams
- 1/8 salt
- 2 ½ tablespoons olive oil
- 4 eggs
- 2 ½ tablespoons oregano
- 1 tablespoons water
- ¼ fresh cilantro
- ¼ tablespoon paprika
- 1/8 tablespoon black pepper
- 1 ounce parmigiano-reggiano
- 1 clove garlic
- 1 medium onion

DIRECTIONS

1. Preheat the oven to 325 F.

2. Put the yam in the oven and roast for 20-25 minutes.

3. When ready, remove and place in a large bowl and mash it with a fork.

4. Heat olive oil in a skillet over high heat and add garlic.

5. Cook for 1 minute and then add onions.

6. Add the mashed yams over onions and fold together.

7. Whisk together the cilantro, water, oregano, salt, paprika, eggs and pepper.

8. Add the egg mixture to the pan and fold the eggs with the onion.

9. Cook for 20-25 minutes.

Nutritional Facts

Amount Per Serving

Calories 390	Calories from Fat 145
	% Daily Value
Total Fat 16g	26%
Saturated Fat 5g	24%
Monounsaturated Fat 7g	
Trans Fat 0g	
Cholesterol 432mg	145%
Sodium 525mg	22%
Total Carbohydrates 17g	6%
Dietary Fiber 6g	22%

Sugars 5g	
Protein 19g	
Vitamin A 19%	Vitamin C 41%
Calcium 28%	Iron 16%
Vitamin K 8 mcg	Potassium 1207 mg
Magnesium 53 mg	

TROPICAL MELON SMOOTHIE

Serves: **1**
Prep Time: **5**   minutes
Cook Time: **10**   minutes
Total Time: **15**   minutes

INGREDIENTS

- 6 ounces cantaloupe
- ½ banana
- ½ cup non-fat yogurt
- 1/3 cup mango

DIRECTIONS

1. Place the melon, banana, mango and yogurt in a blender.
2. Blend until smooth.

Nutritional Facts

Amount Per Serving

Calories 217	Calories from Fat 6
	% Daily Value
Total Fat 1g	1%
Saturated Fat 0g	1%

Monounsaturated Fat 0g		
Trans Fat 0g		
Cholesterol 5mg		1%
Sodium 115mg		5%
Total Carbohydrates 47g		16%
Dietary Fiber 3g		11%
Sugars 39g		
Protein 9g		
Vitamin A 78%	Vitamin C 96%	
Calcium 28%	Iron 5%	
Vitamin K 4 mcg	Potassium 790 mg	
Magnesium 52 mg		

BUTTERNUT SQUASH RISOTTO

Serves: **4**
Prep Time: **15**   minutes
Cook Time: **45**   minutes
Total Time: **60**   minutes

INGREDIENTS

- 2 lbs butternut squash
- 1 cup low sodium chicken
- ¼ sherry
- ½ red onion
- 1 cup rice
- ¼ tablespoon salt
- ½ parsley leaves
- 3 cups water
- olive oil(spray)
- 3 tablespoon virgin olive oil
- 1 leek
- ¼ ground paprika
- 1 ½ parmigiano-reggiano
- 1/8 tablespoon black pepper

DIRECTIONS

1. Preheat the oven to 325 F.
2. Slice the squash and remove the seeds.
3. Spray with olive oil and pace in the preheated oven.
4. Roast the squash for 1 hour.
5. Remove from the oven, after it is cool, drain the liquid and place the squash on a cutting board.
6. Peel the skin from the squash.
7. Slice lengthwise at about ¼ inch intervals and then crosswise, to divide into ½ inch cubes.
8. Slice the leek in half, separating the white from the green tops.
9. Slice the white part of the leek very thin lengthwise and clean.
10. Heat the olive oil in a sauce pan over high heat.
11. Reduce heat and cook the leek.
12. When the leek is wilted add the red onion, also place the rice in the pan and stir for a couple of minutes.
13. Add the chicken, sherry, 2 cups of water, pepper and salt.
14. Add paprika while cooking.

15. Cook the rice for 25 minutes and add water when is needed.

16. Stir frequently and add Parmigiano-Reggiano until it is melded.

Nutritional Facts

Amount Per Serving

Calories 391	Calories from Fat 50
	% Daily Value
Total Fat 6g	9%
Saturated Fat 2g	11%
Monounsaturated Fat 3g	
Trans Fat 0g	
Cholesterol 7mg	2%
Sodium 460mg	19%
Total Carbohydrates 74g	25%
Dietary Fiber 7g	28%
Sugars 8g	
Protein 12g	
Vitamin A 507% Vitamin C 103%	
Calcium 27%	Iron 27%
Vitamin K 138 mcg	Potassium 981 mg
Magnesium 105 mg	

CAULIFLOWER MAC AND CHEESE

Serves: **4**
Prep Time: **10**   minutes
Cook Time: **45**   minutes
Total Time: **55**   minutes

INGREDIENTS

- 8 ounces white cheddar cheese
- 2 ounces whole wheat
- ½ cup 2% milk
- 9 tablespoons panko breadcrumbs
- 2 ½ tablespoons olive oil
- 12 ounces cauliflower
- 2 eggs
- 6 quarts water

DIRECTIONS

1. Preheat the oven at 375 F and place a skillet in it.
2. Add olive oil to the pan and the cauliflower.

3. Roast for 20 minutes, toss cauliflower every 5 minutes after that remove it from oven.
4. Place some water in a medium pot over high heath.
5. Add the pasta and cook until is ready.
6. Combine the eggs with milk in a sauce pan and whisk until smooth.
7. Add the cheddar cheese and salt.
8. When the pasta is done, drain well and add it to the sauce pan.
9. Stir until the cheese is melted.
10. Add the cauliflower and fold together.
11. Place mac and cheese in oven bowls.
12. Top with pepper and sprinkle 2 tablespoons of panko.
13. Put it under the boiler for 2-3 minutes.

Nutritional Facts

Calories 452	Calories from Fat 126
	% Daily Value
Total Fat 14g	
Saturated Fat 5g	20%
Monounsaturated Fat 7g	
Trans Fat 0g	
Cholesterol 59mg	20%
Sodium 498mg	22%

Total Carbohydrates 56g	43%
Dietary Fiber 6g	24%
Sugars 5g	
Protein 29g	
Vitamin A 10%	Vitamin C 32%
Calcium 34%	Iron
	17%
Vitamin K 14 mcg	Potassium
	342 mg

Magnesium 73 mg

CREAMY MAC AND CHEESE

Serves: **4**
Prep Time: **5**   minutes
Cook Time: **40**   minutes
Total Time: **45**   minutes

INGREDIENTS

- 1/8 tablespoon black pepper
- ½ cup 2% milk
- 8 ounces wheat penne pasta
- 1/8 salt
- 2 large eggs
- 5 ounces cheddar cheese
- 4 quarts water

DIRECTIONS

1. Place the water in a pot over high heat.
2. Add the pasta and cool until done.
3. Combine the eggs and milk in a sauce pan and whisk until smooth.
4. Add cheddar cheese and salt.
5. Add pasta to the pot with the cheese over low heat.

6. Stir until cheese is melted.

7. Add black pepper if needed and serve hot.

Nutritional Facts

Amount Per Serving		
Calories 310	Calories from Fat 56	
		% Daily Value
Total Fat 6g		10%
Saturated Fat 3g		14%
Monounsaturated Fat 2g		
Trans Fat 0g		
Cholesterol 117mg		39%
Sodium 344mg		14%
Total Carbohydrates 45g		19%
Dietary Fiber 5g		19%
Sugars 2g		
Protein 21g		
Vitamin A 4%	Vitamin C 1%	
Calcium 22%		Iron 15%
Vitamin K 0 mcg		Potassium 233 mg
Magnesium 95 mg		

CREAMY MUSHROOM MAC AND CHEESE

Serves: **2**
Prep Time: **15**   minutes
Cook Time: **25**   minutes
Total Time: **40**   minutes

INGREDIENTS

- 3 tablespoons olive oil
- 1 egg
- ¼ cup 2% milk
- 2 ½ ounces cheddar cheese
- 8 ounces crimini mushrooms
- 1/8 salt
- 2 ½ tablespoons cornstarch
- 1 ounce dried mushrooms
- 4 quarts water
- 4 ounces whole wheat

DIRECTIONS

1. Preheat the oven to 325 F and place a skillet in it.
2. Add water in a pot over high heat.

3. Remove ½ cup of the water and pour over the dried mushrooms.

4. Add the pasta to the boiling water and cook until done.

5. Place the olive oil in a skillet.

6. Add the crimini mushrooms to the skillet and place it in the oven.

7. Combine the eggs and milk in a sauce pan and whisk until smooth.

8. Add cheddar cheese and salt.

9. Drain the liquid from the mushrooms and add the reconstituted mushrooms to the skillet in the oven.

10. When pasta is done, drain them and add to the saucepan (with the cheese).

11. Stir until cheese is melted.

12. Add the cornstarch to the mushroom broth and mix.

13. Add the cornstarch mixture to the cheese sauce.

14. Cook for 1-2 minutes and then remove from the heat.

Nutritional Facts

Calories 444	Calories from Fat 105
	% Daily Value

	% Daily Value
Total Fat 11g	19%
Saturated Fat 5g	14%
Monounsaturated Fat 5g	
Trans Fat 0g	
Cholesterol 118mg	41%
Sodium 447mg	19%
Total Carbohydrates 64g	19%
Dietary Fiber 8g	26%
Sugars 5g	
Protein 29g	

Vitamin A 4%	Vitamin C 2%
Calcium 32%	Iron 22%
Vitamin K 3 mcg	Potassium 1016 mg

Magnesium 131 mg

EGGPLANT AND GARLIC SOUP

Serves: **4**
Prep Time: **15**   minutes
Cook Time: **65**   minutes
Total Time: **80**   minutes

INGREDIENTS

- 24 ounces eggplant
- 2 ounces goat cheese
- 1 cup water
- 2 tablespoons olive oil
- 1 15 ounce white beans
- 1 bulb garlic
- ½ salt
- black pepper

DIRECTIONS

1. Preheat the oven to 325 F.
2. In a skillet add 2 teaspoons of olive oil.
3. Place the eggplant in the skillet and place it in the oven.
4. Place the garlic in a sauce pan and add the remaining olive oil.

5. Place the garlic in the oven.

6. Roast the eggplant and the garlic for 30-35 minutes.

7. Remove and let it cool.

8. Place everything in a blender.

9. Remove the garlic and also place it in the blender.

10. Add salt, goat cheese and white beans.

11. Serve it!

Nutritional Facts

Amount Per Serving

Calories 224	Calories from Fat 46
	% Daily Value
Total Fat 4g	8%
Saturated Fat 3g	12%
Monounsaturated Fat 1g	
Trans Fat 0g	
Cholesterol 11mg	4%
Sodium 372mg	15%
Total Carbohydrates 34g	15%
Dietary Fiber 13g	44%
Sugars 4g	
Protein 14g	
Vitamin A 4%	Vitamin C 19%

Calcium 14%	Iron 16%
Vitamin K 6 mcg	Potassium 814 mg
Magnesium 82 mg	

EGGPLANT INVOLTINI

Serves: 2
Prep Time: 5   minutes
Cook Time: 60   minutes
Total Time: 65   minutes

INGREDIENTS

- 2 cups tomato sauce
- 1 ounce Parmigiano-Reggiano
- 1 large eggplant
- 4 ounces fresh mozzarella
- 2 ½ tablespoons basil leaves
- black pepper

DIRECTIONS

1. Take a skillet and place it over medium heat and spray it with oil.
2. Add the sliced eggplant and cook for 10 minutes until done.
3. Spray the top of the eggplant sliced and cook for 10 minutes.
4. Remove everything and place it on a paper towel.

5. Preheat the oven to 325 F.

6. Put the mozzarella in a bowl and add basil and pepper.

7. Add 2 tablespoons of the mozzarella mixture on each of the slices of eggplant.

8. Cover the eggplant rolls with tomato sauce.

9. Place the dish in the oven and cook it for 15-20 minutes.

10. Top with the parmesan.

11. Cook for 4-5 minutes.

Nutritional Facts

Amount Per Serving		
Calories 319	Calories from Fat 160	
		% Daily Value
Total Fat 18g		27%
Saturated Fat 9g		34%
Monounsaturated Fat 7g		
Trans Fat 0g		
Cholesterol 45mg		15%
Sodium 624mg		26%
Total Carbohydrates 20g		10%

Dietary Fiber 9g		28%
Sugars 9g		
Protein 22g		
Vitamin A 10%	Vitamin C 29%	
Calcium 65%		Iron
		8%
Vitamin K 15 mcg		Potassium
		821 mg

Magnesium 67 mg

FETTUCCINE ALFREDO – COUMADIN-FRIENDLY VERSION

Serves: **2**
Prep Time: **15**   minutes
Cook Time: **60**   minutes
Total Time: **75**   minutes

INGREDIENTS

- 2 tablespoons olive oil
- 4 ounces whole wheat
- 1 tablespoon parsley
- ¾ cup 2% milk
- 2 cloves garlic
- 1-ounce goat cheese
- 1 ounce Parmigiano-Reggiano
- 4 quarts water
- 3 tablespoons white flour

DIRECTIONS

1. Heat the olive oil in a skillet over medium heat.

2. Add the roasted garlic.

3. Cook slowly and stir frequently.

4. Add the flour slowly and cook for about 1 minute

5. Add the milk slowly, whisking, until the sauce is smooth.

6. Add the goat cheese.

7. When the sauce is smooth, add the Parmigiano-Reggiano.

8. Reduce heat to very low.

9. Heat the water to a boil in a large pot

10. Cook the fettuccine for about 15 minutes.

11. Drain and add the pasta to the sauce.

12. Serve with minced parsley over the top.

Nutritional Facts

Amount Per Serving

Calories 390	Calories from Fat 107
	% Daily Value
Total Fat 12g	19%
Saturated Fat 6g	30%
Monounsaturated Fat 5g	
Trans Fat 0g	
Cholesterol 25mg	8%
Sodium 337mg	14%

Total Carbohydrates 53g		18%
Dietary Fiber 5g		20%
Sugars 5g		
Protein 20g		
Vitamin A 7%	Vitamin C 11%	
Calcium 36%	Iron 16%	
Vitamin K 33 mcg	Potassium 354 mg	
Magnesium 109 mg		

Thank you for reading this book!

Printed in Poland
by Amazon Fulfillment
Poland Sp. z o.o., Wrocław